How To Buy A Great Used Car With Cash

A Simple System for Buying Smart, Avoiding Scams, and Keeping More of Your Cash

Eric Bowie
(Smart Money Bro)

DEDICATION

For the Mendences (Bill and Erika)—whose search for a better car in 2019 inspired me to write this book.

CONTENTS

INTRODUCTION

Take a deep breath, close your eyes, smile slightly, and imagine a life with no car payments. What comes to mind? Peace, serenity, tranquility, and sheer awesomeness! Keep your eyes closed. Now imagine the extra money you have in your pocket, in your savings account, and in your investment portfolio. Imagine how much money you can amass, the vacations, the better quality of life, and the joys of knowing that car is yours and there is no bank, or repo man that can take it away.

Ok, you can open your eyes now. Back to reality. This exercise is a fun thing to do. The reality is that you can actually have that peace if you follow the information embedded in this book. I don't want to sell you a dream but I do want to introduce you to a new reality that can be yours.

This book is all about specific techniques that you can use to purchase good quality used cars for cash.

Many of you may be saying:

"I want a reliable vehicle."
"I don't know anything about cars."
"I don't have the money to buy a car with cash."
"I don't want a lemon."
"Where do I start?"
"Can I really get a good used car with cash?"

These are the types of statements and questions that you are likely pondering over as you delve into this book. That's good. Stay right there in that state of flux as you begin this journey. These are precisely the types of statements we want to address, and the types of questions that we want to answer for you throughout the course of this book. The goal of this book is to send you away with a guide to direct your path to not only help you purchase a used car with cash today, but to make it a cornerstone for how you purchase cars for the rest of your life.

Cherish this book, make notes, write in it, bookmark specific pages, and feel free to carry it with you and use it over the course of your lifetime. This book is a timeless guide to managing the process of purchasing good solid used cars in a way that is economical and thoughtful with your money, specifically with cash!

Everything in this book is meant to provide you with information, give you usable and practical ideas, and empower you with new creative techniques.

This book is your blueprint, your guide, and your handbook.

So, why am I writing this book? I am not a mechanic, but I did work at Jiffy Lube for 2 years when I was 20 years old. And I have spent 30 years buying cars with loans and with cash. I know a thing or two because I've seen a thing or two. At the end of the book, I will go through the history of my car buying experiences for you, which should give you a good idea of my experiences with purchasing cars.

Fortunately, this book is a culmination of all of those years and experiences of car buying. The principles in this book will serve you well whether you buy a new car that is financed with a loan or you buy a used car with cash. My suggestion to you is to ALWAYS buy your cars with cash, but if you choose to buy a car with a loan, you can do it using the techniques I show you!

CHAPTER ONE
PLANNING BEFORE YOU PURCHASE

When you buy a car, it's incredibly important that you walk away from that transaction feeling comfortable with your decision and confident about your purchase. With over 30 years of buying cars—both with loans and with cash—I simply want to give you advice that will help ease your mind and help you feel good about your car-buying decision with your hard-earned cash. In order to do this, you must plan for this purchase.

For most of us, there should be months—and maybe even years—of saving and preparing that go into the decision to make a cash purchase of a vehicle. Buying a car with cash should **not** boil down to an emergency purchase you have to make next weekend. If that happens to you, you've sort of lost before you even started. So here's how you avoid that.

Every good decision you will ever make with money will ALWAYS require foresight on your part. It's an old cliché, but it's incredibly true: *If you fail to plan, then plan to fail.* People who do well with money can see 3, 5, even 10 years down the road. People who do poorly with money often can't see past Friday night. The fact is you will need another car at some point—so save your money now.

When you plan properly to make a car purchase with cash, you put yourself in a position to cut through all of the chase, look past the dog-and-pony shows, and forego the sales pitches you know are coming. The planning phase of your car-buying experience is the beginning of your due diligence and should not be taken lightly or overlooked.

You MUST be willing to do the work, and that work starts long before you make your purchase. If you aren't willing to put in the time, effort, and discipline to plan and save your money, then you probably aren't ready to buy a car with cash. This takes a substantial amount of preparation on your part. The more work you do at this stage, the better chance you have of getting a good deal on a reliable used car and spending your money wisely.

Everyone takes risks, but calculated risks—through good, well-thought-out planning—will lower your risks every time. Put in the work and you will be rewarded. Half-step it and you will pay the price, literally and figuratively. If you are willing to put in the work, you are much less likely to suffer the same fate as people who never prepare.

It's better to take educated, informed guesses than stabs in the dark. That's the premise of planning for a cash car purchase, because it will lower your risks significantly. The biggest hope is that you won't be in an emergency situation when buying your car. If you are, that's okay—this book will help you—but if you plan ahead, you won't have to rush into decisions you wouldn't normally make. The most important thing you must plan for is saving enough cash to purchase a good used car.

Save Before You Shop

If you currently have a car that's still in decent working condition, then plan to save as much money as possible before your next purchase. At some point, we all must make the decision about when to stop throwing money at an old clunker that isn't worth it and put that money toward our next car. That's a personal choice, but when repairs start costing almost as much as the car is worth, it's time to reconsider. If you can save the money you need *before* you get to that point—great! If you can't, then you'll have to decide when it's the right time to give up on the clunker and put that money toward your next purchase.

There's a very clear reason that the first chapter in this book is about planning. You have to get this part of the process down. Positive things happen when you plan and save ahead of time. Everything else in this book becomes far more effective if you are *not* in a desperate situation with very little money to work with.

If you don't plan properly, you'll find yourself at a local auction hoping and praying, or scrolling through online listings hoping and praying, or asking friends and family—still hoping and praying. There's nothing wrong with hoping, and there's nothing wrong with praying; but I'd rather you hope, pray, and prepare ahead of time. Remember, when you work with money, on any level, you MUST PLAN and think about the future.

Use Timing to Your Advantage

If you can avoid buying a car between February and May, do so. Sellers know tax-return season brings thousands of buyers into the market, and they raise prices during that time. Yes, this was true years ago—and it's still true in 2026.

Also, if you're buying from a dealership, the end of the year can still be a good time to catch price drops. There are always deals to be found, but you must stay aware of timing. If you have the freedom to choose *when* to buy, use timing to your advantage.

Just because you have $10,000 saved doesn't mean you have to buy a $10,000 car. If your aunt, coworker, or a trusted friend offers you a good vehicle for less, do your due diligence and make the smart move. Putting leftover cash aside for your next purchase puts you ahead of the game.

Most of the time, there is a noticeable difference between a $8,000 car and an $12,000 car. If you can be patient and save a little more, your quality level usually goes up. If you don't want to study cars, research cars, and learn cars, then you're going to need more money. Your chances of getting a better car almost always increase when you increase your cash.

The entire process of planning your purchase can take anywhere from a few days to a few months of preparation. Be ready. Be patient. Be focused. Everything depends on your willingness to put time and effort into this.

Reduce Your Risk

Buying a used car can feel like a gamble, especially in today's market, but if you prepare properly—if you're willing to learn and take the necessary precautions—you can mitigate your risks and get it done.

If you grew up anything like me, you understand the importance of stretching a dollar. I want your cash to stretch as far as possible in 2026. That means planning, saving, preparing, and putting in the work.

Cash gives you power—but only when paired with wisdom and preparation.

There is more to come in the next chapters. Stick with me, stay committed, and stay prepared.

CHAPTER TWO
CASH IS STILL KING

Should you buy a vehicle using cash or should you finance your purchase? Even in 2026, with all the new digital payment tools and every dealer encouraging you to "build credit" so that you can be eligible for loans, cash is still king.

We all know the problems associated with credit cards. I have known people who have had a credit card for twenty years and still have a balance; yet, that is the mantra of a vast majority of people today. That same mindset carries directly into car purchases. In a world where the average used-car payment is now over $520 and new-car payments often cross $750 to $800 per month, people are still signing up for long-term loans that eat away at their income.

Yes, cash is still king. When you do anything with cash, you are in control. You call the shots. You dictate the process. And ideally, you can be intentional when you are buying a car. Of course, that is the hope.

Why Car Payments Hold You Back

Convincing you that you should buy cars with cash is a great first step in helping you not become trapped in monthly payments and interest charges. There are many ways to destroy your future wealth. We won't go into every one of them in this chapter, but car payments are one of the biggest wealth-killers in most households.

What we will emphasize is that owning your cars outright is a tremendous relief, not just financially but emotionally. Yes, you still have to maintain the car, but not owing anybody is a powerful feeling. And when you own the car outright, the only thing you need to worry about is whether the car is reliable or has a bad track record—because that's what matters.

All of that is fine, understandable, and important. However, there is still another piece that people don't talk about enough: wealth building. When you avoid car payments, you keep your $500 to $800 a month in your pocket, where it belongs.

If you want to lease vehicles because you like the smell of a new car every two years, that's your decision. But remember that you will pay far more—often tens of thousands more over time—for that new-car smell than you ever would for a good, reliable $10,000 car.

I'm not here to sell you any pie-in-the-sky fluff, but there are plenty of reliable used cars available for inexpensive prices. The challenge is that in 2026, repair costs are higher, labor is more expensive, and dealerships push financing harder than ever. That is why having cash—real cash—still positions you to make smarter choices.

Let me be clear: in the past, books and financial experts used to say things like, "$500 a month invested at 9% becomes nearly a million dollars over 30 years." That was the old example. In 2026, a more reasonable expectation is 7% to

8% long-term returns. Even at that rate, if you invested $500 a month instead of sending it to a lender, you'd still end up with roughly $600,000 to $680,000 over 30 years. That's real money. That's real wealth-building. And that's why this conversation matters.

If you want to consider buying a car with cash, you are going to have to think differently if you want different results than everyone else. Most people keep thinking the same way, and that's why they stay in the same financial situations year after year.

Understanding the Power of Cash

By now, you may be wondering: *How do you buy used cars with cash?* The answer starts right here, in this chapter. Before you ever get to the tactics in Chapters Four and Five, you must first understand the power and importance of cash.

Anyone can buy a quality used car with cash, and it doesn't have to be an expensive car. If you want to buy a car with $2,000, then save $2,000. If you want to buy a car with $8,000, then save $8,000. The principle has not changed in 2026, and it never will: The more cash you have, the more options you have.

Keep in mind, there may be 500 quality cars available at $8,000 and 5,000 quality cars available at $15,000. If you don't see anything worth purchasing with your cash, then you need to save up MORE cash. The more cash you have, the less expertise you will need. If you don't want to become a mechanic or spend countless hours learning cars, the simplest solution is to increase your cash. More money gives you access to newer, cleaner, and better-maintained vehicles.

The fact is, very few people have $15,000 or $20,000 lying around for a cash car purchase. But many people can scrape together $3,000 to $10,000 if they plan and stay disciplined. And in 2026, even with inflation, that's still a strong range for good, reliable cars.

The Power Cash Gives You

It's important to note that the type of due diligence you need to do will depend on how much you can spend. The more you can spend, the newer the car will be, the lower the mileage you'll find, and the more mechanically sound the car will likely be. This is another reason you want to save as much cash as possible.

So when you are buying with cash, you have to have a process that helps you get the best car possible. The right knowledge can make up for the lack of cash. But if you have both knowledge *and* cash, you're in a wonderful position.

If you grew up anything like me, you know the importance of making your money stretch. You want to be willing to put in the work necessary to make that happen. Because when you combine cash with preparation, you increase your confidence—and your options—every time.

Cash is still KING! Save your money, commit to these car-buying strategies, and get your highlighters ready! There is more to come in the next chapters.

CHAPTER THREE
UNDERSTANDING THE MARKET
BEFORE YOU START YOUR SEARCH

Buying a good used car with cash starts long before you meet a seller or take a test drive. It starts with understanding the market. When you know what's happening in the market, you make smarter decisions, you avoid pressure, and you protect your money. This chapter will give you a simple way to understand what you're walking into before you begin your search.

The goal here is not to overwhelm you with data. It's to give you a clear picture of how the market works so you can buy with confidence. When you understand the bigger picture, you won't feel rushed, confused, or misled. You'll know what's normal, what's not, and what to expect as you start looking for the right car.

Why the Market Looks the Way It Does

Used-car prices rise and fall for many reasons. Inventory levels change. Gas prices shift. New car prices go up or down. Some cars hold value longer. Some don't. You don't need to be an expert on any of this, but you do need to know one thing: the market is always moving.

This matters for a cash buyer because cash gives you freedom. When you know what type of market you're in, you can decide whether to act now, wait a little longer, or widen your search. Cash puts you in control, not the seller.

Why Newer Used Cars Cost More Than You Expect

Many buyers are surprised when they see the price of newer used cars. Modern cars have more electronics, more features, and more technology than older vehicles. This makes them more expensive to build, and that cost carries over into the used market.

A car with cameras, sensors, screens, and driver-assist features will usually cost more than an older model without them. These features also make repairs more expensive. As a cash buyer, your job is to understand that a newer used car isn't "overpriced" just because the number is high. The technology inside the car plays a big part in the price.

This doesn't mean you shouldn't buy a newer car. It simply means you should look at the price with clear expectations.

Why Older Cars Hold Value More Than Expected

Years ago, a 10-year-old car used to be cheap. Today, a well-maintained older car can hold value longer. Many older cars are built with simpler parts, fewer electronic systems, and more proven engines. When people want something reliable and affordable, they look for these older models — and that demand keeps prices steady.

As a cash buyer, an older car can be a smart move if it has been cared for. Low-mileage older cars often sell fast, so don't be surprised if the asking prices seem stronger than you expected. The goal is not to find the cheapest car. The goal is to find the right car at the right price.

Why Mileage Isn't the Only Thing That Matters

Many people obsess over mileage, but mileage alone doesn't tell the whole story. A high-mileage car that was serviced on time can be better than a low-mileage car that was neglected. What matters most is how the car was used and how it was maintained.

Here's a simple rule to follow:

A well-maintained car with honest history is usually the smartest buy.

Look for service records, consistent oil changes, and signs the owner took care of the car. Don't let mileage scare you away from a vehicle that has been treated right.

Why Private Sellers Can Ask for More

When you shop online, you'll notice that many private sellers ask for prices that seem higher than what you expect. This happens because private sellers usually aren't in a rush. They set a number and wait for someone who is willing to pay it.

Dealerships turn inventory fast. Private sellers don't. This means a private seller may price their car high at first. Many will lower the price later if the car doesn't sell.

As a cash buyer, patience pays off. Let sellers sit with their price. Many times, they will reach out when they are ready to make a real deal.

Why Inventory Changes Depending on Where You Live

Some areas have plenty of used cars. Some areas don't. Cities usually have more choices than small towns. Warmer states often have cars with less rust. Colder states may have better prices but more wear.

Your location affects:

- what types of cars you'll see
- what condition they're in
- how much people are asking

If your local options are limited, widen your search. When you pay with cash, you can travel a little farther to get a better car for your money. Flexibility is one of your strongest tools.

Why Patience Always Pays Off

The biggest mistake buyers make is rushing. Rushing leads to bad decisions. Rushing makes you overlook problems. Rushing makes you pay too much.

When you buy with cash, you don't have a loan approval deadline. You don't have a monthly payment waiting on you. You don't have pressure. You have time.

Use your time wisely.

Study the market.

Watch how prices move.

See which cars sell quickly and which ones sit.

When you understand the market, you walk into the buying process with confidence — and sellers feel that confidence.

What You Should Do Before You Start Looking

Here are a few simple steps to take before you even start searching for cars:

1. **Set your cash budget.**

Know exactly how much you're willing to spend.

2. **Identify the type of car you need.**

Not want — need. Your lifestyle determines the car.

3. **Study listings for several weeks or more.**

Watch prices. Notice patterns. Learn what's normal.

4. Look at multiple sources.

Use online marketplaces, dealership listings, and local ads.

5. Get comfortable walking away.

This mindset saves more money than any negotiation trick.

These steps give you clarity and set you up for a smoother buying process.

Understanding the market is the foundation of buying a good used car with cash. When you know what's happening around you — prices, inventory, technology, and seller behavior — you won't feel pressured or confused. You'll be in control of the process from start to finish.

CHAPTER FOUR
NEGOTIATING WITH CONFIDENCE

No book on purchasing a car would ever be complete without a discussion about negotiating. Negotiating involves spotting a deal, developing your approach to the deal, assessing and gaining leverage, and closing the deal. You do not have to become a professional negotiator, but you should be comfortable with basic negotiating techniques that will serve you well, if and when you decide to negotiate with the seller. The key is to have confidence and not be intimidated by the person or the process!

In my full-time job, I have spent more than a decade negotiating contracts, and there is nothing more important than having a few simple tools and rules of thumb under your belt when you need to negotiate for what you want.

I negotiate with sellers just about everywhere I go, and my wife hates it, but you'd be shocked if you knew how many deals I get, percentages off merchandise and services, and discounts I receive whenever I purchase anything. Whether I'm in a thrift store, a restaurant, or a convenience store, there is always a potential for a deal—a deal that benefits me as a consumer. This is even more true today, with so many sellers posting items—including cars—on online marketplaces where they expect buyers to message back and forth and negotiate just like they would in person.

Everything Is Negotiable

I want to make one thing clear: Everything is negotiable regardless of what any seller tries to tell you. I don't care if someone is selling you a hairbrush, a pillow, this book, or a car – just remember that there is always room for negotiation on anything anyone is attempting to sell. And don't let words like "fixed price," "internet price," or "no-haggle price" intimidate you—many of these numbers are generated by software, inflated for margin, or simply posted to start the conversation.

The first rule of negotiation is to understand that you must be comfortable with the process of going back and forth with a seller over the price for a product. Most people around the world don't have the money to set up a storefront, and tag and track all of their merchandise in a sophisticated computerized software system. People who want to sell their goods put them out, throw a price on the lot and sell their wares individually or in bulk. In most parts of the world, you as the buyer, would go back and forth with the seller until an agreed upon price is reached. You pay them and you walk away with the goods at the agreed upon price. Again, this process of negotiating back and forth is how most of the world does business. Today, this same back-and-forth often happens through text messages or app-based chats, but the dynamic is identical—offers, counters, silence, and leverage still drive the outcome.

In the case of purchasing a car, you must understand that just because a seller places a sticker in the window of a car, it doesn't make that price gospel. I look at the price as simply representing the price point at which the seller wants to start negotiations. Whether or not they decide to reveal it to you, every seller has flexibility on their price. The question is simply whether or not they want to extend any of that flexibility to you. The same logic applies to online listings— algorithms may influence the posted number, but it is still just the seller's starting position, not their final one.

Know What You Want Before You Negotiate

Don't overthink it. Think of it this way: Negotiating anything is simply a matter of first understanding what do you want, having a clear idea of what you can and can't live without, what is the most you will pay, what do you actually want to pay, and what other possible concessions or sticking points that are available to include in the negotiation. It's not rocket science, but it involves thinking in a more strategic manner than you may be used to, or comfortable with. And because so many tools now show price histories, comparable vehicles, and how long a car has been listed, you can prepare more thoroughly than ever before, giving you stronger leverage from the start.

Here are the 6 tactics I use when negotiating car purchases:

1. **Be willing to walk away.** This is the first and absolute most important thing to keep in mind in any

negotiation. Don't lose yourself in the negotiation, and most of all, don't be desperate. Don't enter into any negotiation without the power to walk away. If you can't walk away, you have absolutely no leverage, and you will lose any and every advantage you have. A seller can smell a desperate consumer from a mile away. Be confident and be convinced that the seller needs you more than you need them. I'm not encouraging you to posture or be rude, but I am saying be assured that there are more cars out there, more deals right around the corner, and more possibilities awaiting you. If you ARE desperate, don't act like it. You can still negotiate with the mindset that you can walk away at any time because you can! This applies whether you're negotiating face-to-face or through an online message—don't let the format change your confidence. When you go to purchase your vehicle, if the seller tells you that they absolutely will not negotiate, be prepared to exercise your power to walk away.

2. **Prepare, over prepare, and then prepare some more.** Study and have your ducks in a row. Know what you will and will not accept, and be as ready as possible for the offers you will make and the counteroffers you will likely receive. Be sure to know your absolute highest price you will pay, your best case scenario price you will pay, your must-haves, your items that you want to use as leverage to help

you get a lower price, and your potential concessions. Make use of modern resources—online listings often show price comparisons, market value estimates, and even how many people have viewed or saved the car, all of which strengthen your preparation. In negotiations, preparation will ease your nervousness and set you apart from other buyers. There is no such thing as over preparation.

3. **Be Quiet.** Hush. The less you talk the greater leverage you will have. Or put another way, the less you talk, the slower you lose leverage. Do a lot of listening. In fact, one of your most effective tools is to simply be quiet and listen. Silence will make the seller think. There are times when silence will cause the seller to make a concession or change their price point. Let their offer sit, think on it, and then counter, if necessary. The more you talk, the more you have the opportunity to reveal too much too soon. The same applies when negotiating through text or messaging—quick replies can give away urgency, while a thoughtful pause can create the same pressure silence creates in person. Part of your leverage in negotiations is the fact that the other party doesn't quite know everything you are thinking. Resist the urge to speak up, talk too much, and offer information that does not need to be offered. There is a time to talk, but it's not when you are discussing the price of the car. This leads to #4.

4. **Let them make the first offer that is below their selling price.** Always avoid making the first offer at all cost, and let them make the first offer that is lower than their selling price. Yes, the seller has essentially made the first offer with their selling price, but your job is to ask them for a price they would be willing to sell that is below their asking price. This is especially important today because many listings already show "online discounts" or algorithm-based prices that appear firm, but are not. Don't let preset labels or digital price tags convince you the seller has reached their true bottom line. You can lose a lot by making the first offer! If the seller is selling the car for $5,000, but in their mind, they are willing to sell the car for $4,000, and you offer the seller $4,900, then you just lost $900. You lost $900 simply because you made the first offer.

A good thing to say to a seller is simply "what are you willing to take for this car?" or "what is a price you are comfortable selling the car for?" or "what is the lowest price you are willing to sell the car for?" I may ask it in a manner such as "how flexible are you on the price?" Even in online conversations, these same questions apply—they encourage the seller to reveal flexibility before you anchor yourself too high. What you are doing is testing the seller. Listen closely to how they answer this question. Once they offer, be willing to make a counter offer, but not right away.

5. **Don't be afraid to "ASK."** If you want something, ask for it. Sometimes, when you ask, you will get it. If you are afraid to ask, you will come up short in every negotiation, whether you are on the phone with AT&T and negotiating a new rate for your cable TV services, searching for a bargain at the local Macy's, or embroiled in a high stakes million-dollar negotiation with an overseas company for a high tech software application for your business, you need to be comfortable and confident with the "ask" as you enter into negotiations. And with dealerships increasingly adding "market adjustment" fees, mandatory protection packages, subscription-based features, and other padded costs, asking for these to be removed can dramatically drop your final price. Most buyers never think to ask—and they pay for things they don't even need. I can't stress enough how important this step is. If you don't ask for what you want, you will never receive it!

6. **Go for the Win-Win.** Again, listen to the seller carefully. The more you listen carefully, the better you will be able to meet the needs of the seller. Think of the other party as a partner, not an adversary. Meet the core of their needs, without going lower than your low (which you have already established before the negotiations). In a negotiation, two satisfied parties make for a good night's sleep. You don't have to completely get over on the other party to get a win,

and they don't have to obliterate your budget to get a win from you. At the end of the day, the seller wants to sell for a fair price and you want to purchase a good car at a fair price. Even with all the data, market comparisons, and digital tools at your disposal, the goal is still a fair and respectful negotiation—not crushing the seller. Work to make that happen and negotiations can be both amicable and satisfying. The key here is to be ethical, fair, and reasonable.

CHAPTER FIVE
76 STRATEGIC TACTICS TO BUY THE RIGHT CAR

Buying a used car with cash is powerful, but power doesn't help you unless you know how to use it. The market is full of good cars, bad cars, honest people, and people who will say almost anything to make a sale. Cash protects you, but only when you're patient, observant, and willing to follow proven strategies that keep you from getting caught off guard.

These 76 tactics are simple, practical, and based on real experiences—things that help you avoid mistakes and move through the buying process with confidence. When you use them, you stay in control. You buy on your terms. You avoid unnecessary stress. And most importantly, you protect your money.

Take your time with these tactics.

Apply them one by one.

Let them guide you through the search, the inspection, the negotiation, and everything in between.

When you follow these strategies, you don't just buy a car— you make a wise financial decision that pays off for years to come.

1. Start Saving Before It Sneaks Up on You

As mentioned earlier, plan your attack and start saving your money NOW! Don't wait. You will be buying a car sometime in the near future. Don't let it sneak up on you.

2. Avoid Buying During Tax-Refund Season

If you can avoid buying a car between the months of February and May, do so. The magic time of year for dealers and car sellers is right around the time when people here in America are receiving their annual tax refunds from the government. Sellers are well aware that many people wait to buy cars with their tax refund money between February and May, and they hike up prices during that time of the year. I don't blame them for doing it because it's a smart business move, but you need to be aware of this as a buyer. Private sellers on platforms like Facebook Marketplace now do the same thing and raise prices during tax season, so be aware of this as well. Also, if you buy from a dealer, one of the best times of the year to buy a car is usually towards the end of the year when very few people are buying cars. There are always good deals out there, but beware of the specific times of the year. If you have a choice of when to purchase your vehicle, take this into consideration when deciding when to purchase.

3. Don't Spend Every Dollar You Saved

Just because you have $10,000 saved doesn't mean you have to buy a $10,000 car. If you have $10,000 and your sweet old Aunt Joyce offers you a very nice vehicle for $7,500, do your research and due diligence on the vehicle, and purchase it. Put the extra $2,500 aside for your next cash car purchase.

4. More Cash, Better Car

Most of the time, there is a big difference between a $4,000 car and a $8,000 car. If you have some patience, and save up just a little more, the quality level of the car you purchase will go up! If possible, be patient and save more money, or you can always simply become a mechanic and expert at cars. I'm being a bit sarcastic here, but you get the point: Your chances of getting a better car go up by increasing the amount of cash you have to spend. Because modern cars have far more electronics and safety sensors than they did years ago, the gap in long-term reliability between cheaper and more expensive used cars is even larger today.

5. Commit Fully to the Cash Purchase

Be committed to the cash purchase. Don't waiver. Don't give in when you pass the pay day lenders in the strip mall. Don't call the 1-800 number to get a quick loan. Don't give in to the temptation to respond to the dealership that advertises that they will accept a $500 down payment and "get you in a vehicle today." Regardless of the offer and the temptation, don't do it. Be committed to a cash purchase!

6. Start With People You Know and Trust

Ask family and friends if they, or anyone they know and trust, is selling a car. First, always start with who you know and trust. This tip is one that most people do not use fully. Typically, we ask one or two of our most immediate family members and that's it. The last thing you want to do is buy a car, and find out a month later that your cousin just sold his car which had half the miles on it and for half the price you just paid for your car. I'm telling you to ask cousins, uncles, aunts, friends of friends, co-workers, former co-workers, and other people you are acquainted with. If you have a lot of friends on your Facebook website, ask them. Post that you are looking for a vehicle. This is a good way to get a better deal. Still do your due diligence though! Also check neighborhood apps, private Facebook groups, and community group chats, because many people now sell cars directly to people within local trusted circles.

7. Prioritize How Well It Runs

The one thing that matters most about the car you are purchasing is how well it runs and its ability to get you from point A to point B. The less money you have, the more you MUST stick to this principle. The more money you have, the more choices you have, and the pickier you can be. It is important that you really get this point. Go for a good running car over and above everything else. Make this your priority.

8. Put Needs Above Wants (And Write Them Down)

Prioritize your specific NEEDS first, and then worry about your WANTS later. This is a spinoff of #7 above, but it more specifically says to identify exactly what matters most, and put these things in order. Literally, write everything down. #1, #2, and #3 on your needs list that will take priority. Keep this in mind, or keep it handy, as you start your search for a vehicle.

9. Don't Sweat Small Cosmetic Problems

Don't sweat the small stuff when you find a great, mechanically inclined car. If you have only $2,000 and you happen to find a fantastic running vehicle for $2,000, don't worry about the fact that it's blue and you don't like blue cars. Stop it. The goal is to find a good running car that fits your needs, not a perfect car with all of the bells and whistles. When you buy a used car, there will be things wrong with it.

You have to enter this process realistically. It may have a ding on the door, a scratch on the bumper, or the FM radio may not be working. So what!

10. Define Your Parameters

Know your parameters. Hopefully you've saved enough money to actually have some parameters and choices. Although your primary parameter is the amount of available money you have for the purchase, there may be other parameters you will be considering such as the mileage on the vehicle, a limit on the age of the vehicle, a limit on a specific type of vehicle or a particular make and model. Perhaps you want a Ford because you've had great luck with Fords in the past. If you have the right amount of money and you've planned accordingly, then add Ford to your list of parameters. Perhaps you may want a larger vehicle because you have a large family, so you have to purchase a vehicle that can fit car seats and booster seats. The point here is to develop your reasonable and practical parameters that are relevant to your individual situation. This is not in contradiction to #7 or #8 above. Your parameters are not necessarily "needs" but if you've done the planning and proper saving, it's ok to have some "wants" or parameters. Of course, if you haven't done the proper planning, then these parameters will have to take a backseat to what you need.

11. Begin Your Search Online

Begin the next phase of your search online (e.g. craigslist.org, cargurus.com, autotrader.com, cars.com, etc.). Outside of your family and friends, this is the next place to begin your search. It's not the only place to look, but if you have an opportunity to begin your search online, it's a good place to start. It will give you an idea of what cars cost, what's out there in the market, and how far your dollar "may" take you in your car search. Also be sure to check Facebook Marketplace, which has become one of the main places private sellers list vehicles today.

12. Make Calls and Take Organized Notes

Make calls. Make a list of the information about the cars that you receive from each call. If you are interested in a vehicle, document the phone number, person you talked to, year make and model, mileage, how long the car's been for sale, is it a one owner or multiple owners, does it have a clean Carfax or had body damage from accidents, is it a clean title or not, is it a car dealership or a personal dealer or an individual seller, and any special notes. Also record how you feel about the car. Sounds like a lot, but it's necessary to be organized throughout this process. Also, keep in mind that every dealership has a website. You can check there as well for cars. This phone call is crucial. Again, keep yourself as organized as possible throughout the process. If the seller is online, also screenshot or save the listing because some scammers delete and repost frequently.

13. Ask Lots of Questions to Reveal the Truth

Always be aware of the fact that there are some folks that sell cars who are not 100% truthful. Shocker, right? Seriously, the best way to find out if a person is being untruthful is to ASK LOTS OF QUESTIONS! If the person you are calling doesn't want to answer your questions, move on. When you cold call a person, primarily an individual seller, your easiest way to reduce risks is to ask questions until you are satisfied that this is a person you can do business with. If you ask enough questions, it can help you learn more about the car and learn more about the person selling the car. The more you know about a purchase, the more leverage you will have if you are serious about this being the car that you want to buy. If the seller becomes evasive or changes details from the online listing, treat that as a major red flag.

14. Trust Your Intuition

If you get a bad vibe on a phone call, move on. Period. Don't play around with this one. Your intuition should not be ignored. God gave us intuition for a reason. Don't try to reason it away. If you have a phone conversation, ask all of your questions, and if you simply don't feel good about pursuing this particular car or going to the next step with this seller, don't do it. If something inside of you is telling you "something ain't right," then something is not right. After you call on a few cars, this will become easier and easier to do. Your ability to discern will get better when you use it. This is even more important now because many scams are designed to pressure or confuse buyers—your intuition can help you avoid them.

15. Never Buy Without Seeing It in Person

Never buy a car without looking at it in person first! There are numerous online ways to buy a car, but please, whatever you do, look at each and every car you are interested in purchasing, in person. And by the way, you'll have plenty of time to fall in love with a car, but don't fall in love with a car based on a picture on the internet, or because the seller sounds kind, or nice, or trustworthy! Anything you are going to drop your hard earned cash on, you must see it in person. Some of you won't buy a $10 shirt without seeing it in person and trying it on, so don't spend thousands on a vehicle without doing that same "in-person" due diligence. Pictures can be edited, filtered, or cropped to hide damage today, so in-person verification is more essential than ever.

16. Don't Be Afraid to Travel Outside Your City

While you are doing this search, don't be afraid to travel an hour or more from where you are currently located to view and buy a vehicle. If you are in a larger city, some of your best deals can be found just outside your major city in the more rural areas, an hour or two from your city. So plan to drive around neighborhoods on the outskirts of any major town. These vehicles for sale, oftentimes, never make Craigslist and other conventional ways of being advertised. There is a 60+ year old couple looking to get rid of a well taken care of 6-year-old Buick Century 20 miles outside of every city in America. These can be fantastic deals to snag. Many good private-owner cars are sold locally through yard signs or local bulletin boards and never appear online.

17. Never Go Alone When Viewing Cars

Never go to look at cars alone. Be safe in the process, take at least one other person with you, and proceed with your car search with caution and safety. If it's someone that is knowledgeable about cars, great. If they aren't as knowledgeable, that is ok. The whole point with this tip is that you don't want to be alone. With that said, don't bring your whole crew. That is not necessary either. You are out looking for cars and you don't need the distraction of 5 family members or even 4 friends. Attention and laser-like focus are crucial in this process. If you can, leave the family and children at home. Bring one or two essential people to help you decipher information, discern information, see things you may not see, and keep yourself safe in this process. Meeting in public places with cameras, such as a police station parking lot, adds an extra layer of safety.

18. Take Notes While You Look at Cars

When you go looking for cars, ALWAYS bring a pen and a piece of paper and take notes, or take notes on your phone. I'm a bit old-fashioned, so I like to bring my list and a pen and paper. You cannot remember everything. Trust me when I tell you this. When you go out and spend the day looking at cars, you have to have a system to keep your notes in order. No better way than to write it down or use your phone to take copious notes. Look, you won't remember all of this information the first few times you look at vehicles, so trust me when I tell you that it is vital that you TAKE DETAILED NOTES! Taking photos or short videos of each car can also help you remember key details later.

19. Be Open to Seeing Other Cars the Seller Has

Feel free to ask buyers if they have other cars that fit your parameters. If it's a dealership they will give you their sales pitch. You really don't want it. Be respectful and listen, but in your mind, you want to sort of get the most crucial information. Respectfully, cut through the chase and look at the other cars, and examine what you are there to examine. Take care of business, but be open to looking at other cars that they may have available. Some small used-car sellers rotate inventory quickly, so checking what just arrived that day can give you early access to good finds.

20. Always Ask How Long the Vehicle Has Been for Sale

Always ask sellers how long they've had the vehicle for sale. A savvy seller will always underplay this and shoot you a low number because they know that is an inquiry by you to figure out your leverage. Always remember, YOU ARE PLAYING CHESS while the average seller is normally playing checkers. If the car has been for sale for a long time (i.e. months), then

41

you have leverage as a buyer, if the seller wants to sell the car as soon as possible. Conversely, if the car has only been for sale for 5 days, you have less leverage. Think about this from a seller's standpoint. If my asset has only been for sale for 5 days, then I'm less likely to take less than if it's been for sale for 5 months. So knowing how long it's been on the market is information you want to know. Some online platforms display "time listed," so verify the seller's answer against the listing when possible.

21. Ask How Flexible They Are on Price

Always ask the seller how flexible they are on the price. A seller's answer to this question, and HOW they answer this question means a lot! It's not a deal breaker if they aren't flexible on the price. You ask this question because it may give you a glimpse of how negotiations will go, if and when, it comes to negotiating. Some sellers will say "I'm flexible." Many will also say, "I'm not that flexible on the price." How they answer this question will give you information you want. Be sure that you ask this question in front of the person you brought with you. You both want to be able to see the seller's reaction to this question. Some people are uncomfortable asking whether or not the seller is flexible on their price, but you are exercising your right to know, and it's your right and duty to ask! After all, you are trying to get a good deal and you can't be shy. On online listings, a long time without price drops may also indicate how flexible or inflexible a seller is.

22. Use Car-Buying Apps

Don't forget about car buying apps such as Letgo or OfferUp. These apps, along with others, can be downloaded on your phone for easy access to lots and lots of cars for sale. The point is to use whatever current technological source that is available for you to find vehicles for sale. If you are reading this book in 2030 or 2040, there will be other avenues for you to find cars for sale. Take advantage of whatever technology is out there, to help you locate and source cars for sale. Letgo no longer exists in many regions, and OfferUp has become much more common, but the main platform most private sellers now use is Facebook Marketplace. Use it heavily during your search.

23. Don't Take Abuse From Sellers

As a buyer, you do not have to take any abuse. I don't care if you have $1,500 or $15,000, don't stand for rude or disrespectful behavior from a seller. You have planned the purchase, you are wise and intelligent, and you don't deserve to be treated like you are doing the seller a favor. You have the money and they should be working to get your business. NEVER take any abuse from a seller that should be trying to get your money. Regardless, be willing to walk away. Most sellers know that if you leave their car without making a deal, the chances of you returning are low! And they are right! So you have the leverage in this scenario. Many sellers online may act short or dismissive through messages; treat this the same as in-person disrespect and move on.

24. Don't Carry Large Amounts of Cash While Shopping

Never carry all of your cash with you when you go looking at cars. You leave yourself open to getting robbed or losing your money. You should always have access to your cash, just in case you find something immediately, but don't carry large amounts of cash. It's simply not wise nor smart to do this! Use a bank branch, credit union, or secure digital method to finalize payment only after you decide to buy.

25. Be Willing to Walk Away From Any Car

Always be willing to walk away from any car, even one that you really like. If you can't walk away, you are buying on emotion, and not on logic, and you are subject to feeling that you have no options. When you have no options, you significantly increase your risks of making bad decisions. This means you can't fall in love with a car, fawn over a car, or get gushy feelings over a car. You are buying a car, not a girlfriend, not a boyfriend, and not a best friend. Cars don't have feelings. Make the purchase based upon logic and common sense. Don't become attached to a vehicle. If you aren't willing to walk away from a car, you set yourself up for a loss in this process. Online buying makes this even easier— there are thousands of cars for sale at any moment, so never feel locked into one option.

26. Act Confident (Even If You Aren't Yet)

Act confident – You may not be confident yet, but act like it. The seller never has to know what you don't know. If you approach your purchase with the information I'm giving you in this book, you WILL be confident, and you gain confidence along the way. You will be shocked at how people talk to you and treat you when you act confident, ask questions, and carry yourself in a confident way. The whole point here is to present yourself in a confident manner. By the time you look at car number 3 or 4, and so on, you will be more confident. You will soon be able to sniff through the bad stuff and pick up clues and begin to see and hear things that you never noticed. Play chess. The other point here is that you will only have to "act" confident for a short period of time. Again, when you do this for a minute, you will be confident and it won't be an "act" anymore. Confidence also helps prevent sellers—especially online—from trying to rush, pressure, or intimidate you.

27. Speak Less, Listen More

When you first meet a seller, you don't have to say much. It's better to be quiet so that no one knows you don't know what you are doing, then to open your mouth and expose that you don't know what you are doing. In other words, speak less, listen more, because silence can say a lot and it reveals nothing. In other words, confidence is quiet and it's not loud, flashy, arrogant, or boisterous. When you go to view a car, the less you talk the more leverage you keep. The first thing

45

some sellers will do when you talk very little, is talk a lot! Let them talk while you just listen. Trust me. It works. If you get a seller that doesn't talk much, be leery. They are trying to sell you a car for $5,000 and they won't tell you about it? Why not? What are they hiding? You are making a purchase of a car and the more you can listen and learn about the car, the better. Don't get out there talking just to hear yourself talk. This applies online too   don't overshare in messages; let the seller reveal more than you do.

28. Use Small Talk Strategically

Make meaningful, yet strategic small talk with a seller at first, and again, listen very carefully. A seller will usually provide clues in what they are saying. Sometimes you will find something out that you like, or don't like. Believe it or not, this matters! Pay attention to the seller. Sometimes an uncomfortable seller is a seller that is not confident with the car they are selling. Sometimes an uncomfortable seller is an indication they are not being forthcoming with important information about the car that should be disclosed. You can learn a lot through simple strategic mundane conversation. The seller is watching you and will sometimes make small talk with you. That is ok and fine. The whole point here is to get the seller to talk. The more a seller talks, the more they reveal about themselves, the history of the car, their motives, the problems with the car, and other pertinent information that you can use in your decision making process. Even in online chats, how a seller communicates—rushed, vague, or overly talkative—can reveal details about the situation and the car.

29. Use Google and YouTube to Educate Yourself

Google and YouTube can be your best friends on this journey. Use them! This tip goes hand in hand with #55 on this list. This is a very important step but it requires some work on your part. This doesn't take a whole lot more time and effort than what you already spend on Facebook or Instagram every single day. Replace that time with researching gaskets, oil pans, tie rods, bushings, rear seal leaks, transmission leaks, and other things you may find under the bottom of a vehicle. This stuff may be of little or no interest to you, but remember, you are about to spend thousands of your hard earned dollars, so learn just a tad bit about what you are going to purchase and what to look for in the process. Read articles to learn what to look for and what to consider when buying a car. If you see a car you like in your search, research the recalls on the vehicle, research the consumer reports on the vehicle, and research what owners have said about the vehicle you are looking at. This is HUGE!!! There are now free VIN-scanner apps and recall-check tools that make this research even easier and faster.

30. Educate Yourself About Basic Car Knowledge

You don't have to be an expert mechanic, but you should educate yourself about general information about cars. If you can watch the latest episode of Grey's Anatomy, then you can surely take a few minutes out of your day to begin to learn about something you are about to spend lots of money on. Short videos on TikTok and YouTube now explain basic car components in simple ways, making this even easier than before.

31. Consider Looking at Multiple Cars in One Day

If possible, try to look at 2 or 3 cars in the same day. This is a strategy that will really improve your ability to compare and contrast cars. If you look at a car on Monday and the next car on Saturday, for example, you immediately lose the benefits of comparison. You simply won't remember everything about the Monday car on Saturday. If possible, look at multiple cars in a single day. That gives you a basis for comparison and it keeps the previous comparison fresh in your mind. You can also learn more simply because you are "in the moment" and you remember more. If you're searching online, also try to schedule multiple viewings back-to-back so you remain in a focused mindset and avoid forgetting details.

32. Keep Your Notes Organized

Be sure to keep your notes organized. Again, this is similar to #18 on this list. When you get back in the car to leave, take the time to organize your notes on each car. This is crucial to do and you want to be taking these notes IMMEDIATELY after you see a car. If a particular car is a definite "NO," or a "NEVER," then make sure that is the first thing you write down. This is the time to transcribe everything you recall. Remember, if you do this for several days or several weeks or months, your notes will increase, and this process can quickly become overwhelming, unless you keep your notes tight and orderly. If you use your phone, create a separate note or folder for each car so details don't get mixed up.

33. Slow Down and Take Your Time

Take your time going through your search process. Yes, take your time, because when you buy a vehicle, you don't want to regret your choice. When you are using cash, it's important that you buy with confidence. You want as many choices and options as possible. Take your time and make an informed decision throughout the process. Every step of searching and shopping should be done deliberately and with very little emotion. DO NOT RUSH THE SEARCH PROCESS! Rushed decisions are where most buyers get taken advantage of, especially in online marketplaces where sellers may push for quick decisions.

34. Look Around the Vehicle Before Touching Anything

When you get inside a vehicle for the first time, go to the passenger side and look around without touching anything. Watch the person you've brought with you check the fluid under the hood first. That is what they should be doing anyhow. Wherever you look, don't touch. Just plan to sit inside the car without touching anything. Quietly sit there while your partner inspects the fluids underneath the hood. You want to allow your partner some time to investigate under the hood and for yourself to quietly observe the inside of the vehicle with your eyes first, and don't touch anything yet. This quiet first look can help you spot things sellers try to hide, such as strong air fresheners masking odors or odd dashboard lights.

35. Look at the Dashboard Before Starting the Car

Before you put the key into the ignition and start the car, glance at the dashboard. You want to make sure that there aren't any red flags on the dashboard. Your dashboard may give you clues of potential issues like the check engine light being on, the tire pressure monitoring system light being on, the maintenance required light being on, an anti-lock brake system light being on, or some type of malfunction within the air bag system within the vehicle. Anything that concerns you must be addressed immediately. Ask the seller, "Can you explain this light being on?" Do this before you start the car up and hear it run. Some sellers will intentionally disconnect batteries or clear codes right before you arrive, so ask when the car was last driven or whether the battery was recently changed.

36. Pay Attention to Dashboard Information

Pay attention to the entire dashboard at this moment. Your car's oil pressure, water temperature, and battery voltage are usually displayed on your dashboard, somewhere. Not all cars will display these important pieces of information. If they do display these values, be sure to take a longer look at these parts of the dashboard before starting the car. This is the time to really examine the car with detail, focus, and specificity. If the car has a digital dashboard, scroll through the menus to check for service messages or warnings the seller didn't mention.

37. Start the Engine While Standing Outside

Bring the key to your partner and have them start the car up while you are standing OUTSIDE the car. When that car starts up, listen very closely to how that engine sounds. It can be a very loud sound, or a quiet sound. Listen for any knocks, ticking, humming, or other abnormal sounds. Your ears will pick up the sound of an old engine, a bad miss, a misfire, or the sound of a car that doesn't sound quite right. Stand there and listen! Remember, when an engine starts, it should start up smoothly and quietly. Don't let the seller distract you. Watch and listen to the engine. If the seller insists on starting the car themselves or refuses to let you stand outside to listen, that's a red flag.

38. Pay Attention to How the Car Idles

Pay close attention to how the vehicle idles. WATCH IT IDLE. When you open the hood of a vehicle that is already idling you expect to hear a clean idle. You want to actually hear less. The more idling sound you hear, the more it concerns you. You want to hear a smooth and quieter idle.

51

Sure, older cars usually have louder idles and the engine will be louder on older vehicles, but you really want a smooth and quieter idle sound under the hood of a used vehicle if possible. If the idle fluctuates up and down, or the engine seems to shake, those are signs of underlying issues.

39. Get Under the Hood

Look underneath the hood of the car. You want to first make sure that the fluids are clean and FULL. Next, check for ANY leaks. You want to be aware of leaks under the hood. You don't need to be a mechanic to be able to see that oil is leaking from underneath the motor. Some oil leaks are very slow and will have accumulated old oil around the motor, whereas others will be recent and that too will give you clues. All of this information helps you determine whether or not you have further negotiating room, or if the vehicle should be avoided altogether. Check around the valve cover, oil pan, and timing cover—these are common leak points sellers often try to wipe clean before you arrive.

40. Examine the Coolant Reservoir Carefully

Now take a good look inside the coolant reservoir. Look for any cheap quick fixes. Some people will put stop leak or other similar cheap quick-fix substances into their coolant reservoir. This could indicate bigger issues or potential bigger issues. Make sure to tell the seller they need to explain this to you. A current owner may have owned the car for only 6 or 8 months and they are selling the car quickly, so they don't care about longevity of the vehicle. Some quick-fixes usually don't last long-term. A quick fix in the coolant is a HORRIBLE SIGN when you are buying a used vehicle with cash. Also check if the coolant color looks muddy, mixed with oil, or unusually dark—this can indicate head gasket problems.

41. Look at the Radiator for Leaks and Damage

Now look at the radiator. You want to check for any leaks around the radiator. Sometimes, you can see problems with hoses, or even leakages under the radiator. Sometimes on older radiators you will see areas where they have tried to patch or mend small cracks in the radiator that are fixable short-term but not long-term. All of these are clues for you to determine if this is a good buy or not. The radiator is a major part of the vehicle and a leaking radiator is a bad sign. Most people that sell their cars don't have brand new radiators on them. Parts like a radiator will tell you a lot about the car. If the radiator fins are bent or the radiator support looks damaged, it may also indicate a prior accident even if the seller didn't disclose it.

42. Open the Oil Cap and Inspect for Milky Substances

Next, open the oil cap and look inside of it. You are looking for a greyish or whitish and creamy colored substance in the oil cap. This is a REALLY BAD SIGN and a sign that water or coolant is mixing with the oil due to a blown head gasket or a bad cracked block that is allowing the oil and coolant to mix. If you see this, then the house is on fire and you need to leave RIGHT NOW. Do not go any further with this particular car. Looking in the oil cap gives you valuable insight. And this is the time when you want this insight. THIS IS EXTREMELY IMPORTANT! If the cap is freshly cleaned or the engine looks unusually shiny, be cautious— sellers sometimes wipe evidence away.

43. Check the Dipstick Thoroughly

Next, check the dipstick for the condition of the oil. What you expect to see in the dipstick is oil that is at LEAST the NORMAL expected level. A seller should have checked the oil if they are selling a car. If a seller is careless and irresponsible in checking the oil, then that should be a sign for you that they aren't that conscientious when it comes to maintaining the car. Next, look for consistency of the oil on the dipstick. If the oil looks like it has LOTS of mud in it, or is as thick as mud, then again, the house is on fire and you need to leave RIGHT NOW. You don't want DARKER THAN NORMAL, super cloudy oil either. The oil in the car will depend on the mileage. Newer car buying? Expect cleaner oil from the dipstick. Older engine? Expect darker oil. Overall, you want good oil and oil that is in decent shape on the dipstick. If the dipstick is missing altogether, leave immediately — that's a major red flag.

44. Touch the Dipstick Oil to Check Consistency

When you pull out the dipstick to check the oil, feel it between your fingers. This is necessary because you want to feel if the oil is gritty, gritty AND watery, or some other consistency. You want fairly clean oil (depending on the mileage). What you are doing here is checking the oil for consistency. This is very important and you will be glad you did. If the oil feels extremely thin, it may indicate the seller added lighter oil to mask engine noises.

45. Check Transmission Fluid Levels

Next, check the transmission fluid. If there is NO transmission fluid on the dipstick, the house is on fire and leave RIGHT NOW! A seller should make sure that there is transmission fluid on the dipstick for the automatic transmission. If there is, make sure that the color is NOT brown or dark brown. These darker colors are indicators that the transmission may have poor, or bad, transmission fluid, and this will require some eventual cost to you, if you buy the vehicle. Again, this gives you leverage and can be used in negotiations. You want to use this information for a major advantage when it comes to your negotiating power when it's time to negotiate. Burnt-smelling transmission fluid is also a sign of major future problems—always smell the dipstick.

46. Examine Power Steering Fluid Carefully

Next, check the power steering fluid. You check power steering fluid the same way you check transmission fluid. If you see that it's super cloudy, watery and cloudy, or watery and clear, leave RIGHT NOW. If it is that consistency, then this means that there is water mixing with the power steering fluid. If it's mixing with water somewhere, that's a bad sign. Low power steering fluid can also indicate a leak in the pump or hoses, which can be expensive to repair.

47. Watch for Engine Smoke at Startup

Watch the smoke when the car first starts. White smoke could be water in the exhaust. This could be an indication of a bad head gasket in the car. White smoke can be an expensive fix. A bluish type of smoke could be an oil burn off problem with the vehicle and this is a bad sign that oil is burning through the exhaust. When someone starts a car from a cold start, WATCH THE SMOKE! Ask the seller what the problem is with the exhaust. If they don't tell you, and if they can't explain it, leave RIGHT NOW and don't come back or think about this particular car again. This is a bad sign and is potentially very costly and dangerous. If the seller insists the engine was "just started recently," be cautious—they may be hiding cold-start smoke.

48. Look Under the Car for Leaks and Loose Parts

Check underneath the car. What you are looking for are oil leaks of any kind. Look for ANY leaks; not just oil, but coolant and any other leaking fluids. You also want to check for anything that is lying around the car like screws, bolts, pieces of plastic, and other clues that the car could have a potential problem. If you see lots of junk underneath the car that seems to be out of place, you need to pay careful attention. You want to trust your eyes so listen to what you see. Don't let the buyer distract you at this time. Don't talk very much. Stay focused. Be sure that YOU do this. Don't let the buyer or your partner show you this. You look! You want to discover the clues for yourself. Also check for fresh oil stains on the ground beneath the parking spot—the seller may be parking in a way to hide them.

49. Know the Importance of Oil Leaks

Some leaks are small leaks from a small gasket leak or a water pump leak, and others are major leaks from the rear pinion seal drip, a cracked pan, or compromised seals. Whatever leaks you see, and however small or large they are, write them down, but also make a determination about each leak. Very small leaks such as transmission leaks or front seal leaks can be repaired but they are leaks nonetheless and you need to be conscious of it. Huge leaks that leave stains on the ground underneath should be written down because it can tell you where the leak is from, how bad it is, and it can give you negotiating power on the price. Be aware that some sellers may wipe the bottom of the engine clean before you arrive, so check for fresh wet spots or drips.

50. Look for Signs of Power Steering Leaks

Regarding power steering leaks, note if the power steering fluid is present or not and if it's leaking at all. Keep in mind, some older vehicles may have a small leak which could be related to needing an O-Ring replaced or the power steering hose may need to be replaced. If you hear a sound when you try to turn the wheel, and the sound persists when you turn the wheel, you are hearing signs of a possible power steering leak. Again, use ALL information when making your pending decision on your cash car purchase. Check the ground under the car's front end as well—power steering leaks often drip forward and can be spotted more easily outside than under the hood.

51. Inspect the Brake and Transmission Lines

Next, pay attention to brake lines, transmission lines, radiators, and connecting hoses. Pay attention to EVERYTHING under the hood. Some leaks can be costly depending on what it is. Pay attention to what is leaking or what has the potential to leak in the future. Be very careful here. Some connections and hoses are older and have hairline cracks in them, and some of those cracks cannot be seen in the early stages. Be careful here! If any hoses or lines look freshly cleaned or unusually shiny, the seller may be trying to hide evidence of recent leaks.

52. Consider Going to a Repair Shop With the Seller

Take the car and seller to a car repair shop. Lots of people do not do this part. This step is huge and can save you lots of time, lots of money, and potentially save you from a bad purchase. If a seller has a problem doing this (in general), then move on. Keep in mind, some people are not comfortable going too far from their homes (you'll see a little further down what to do about this situation). However, all things being equal, bringing the car to a mechanic is a crucial step. You want the car to be thoroughly examined. There could be a tiny rubber leak at the very bottom of the transmission but the mechanic will find it. Any respectable mechanic will examine ALL key components of a car. If the seller, dealer, or private party seller is being honest, then they know that people take cars to be looked at by a trustworthy mechanic before purchase. Mobile mechanics are also an option now if the seller refuses to drive far; they can meet you at the seller's location for an inspection.

53. Use the Mechanic's Findings as Leverage

Next, use that trip to the mechanic to further reveal more information about the car. For example: you want detailed information, you want to know ALL of the key information, BEFORE you think about purchasing the car. Take this information and use it as leverage in your negotiations. All of this information becomes helpful for YOU the buyer. The more information you have, the better. Keep in mind, the seller usually has all of the information. A good seller will tell you some of the important things, but not everything. A bad seller will tell you none of the important things, except the good stuff. Car dealers do inspections all the time as well. It's smart to get ALL the information you can get. This information will benefit you in every way. If the mechanic provides a written inspection, save it — this can help justify your offer with proof.

54. Always Test Drive the Car

Test drive the car. You want to test drive the vehicle on several roads and freeways. Take the vehicle at high speeds and low speeds. Braking, acceleration, taking turns, and all other components are important. Don't go too quickly when test driving a car. Take your time. If the seller insists on going on a particular route, don't argue, get on that particular route and then take it upon yourself to go down other roads. Be careful, but don't be scared to take the car where it needs to be taken during a test drive. Your goal is to take your time and thoroughly be aware of the car and ANY potential problems that you may encounter down the road. If the seller refuses to allow a freeway drive, that is another red flag — many major issues only appear at higher speeds.

55. Research the Car Deeply

Research the car that you like. This goes along with #29. If the test drive goes well, and you feel good about everything at this point, go back to research on the car again. Old cars, old collision damage, suspension issues, drive issues, transmission issues, leaks, and the list of potential problems go on and on. These are the things that should keep you researching the car. You want to research the heck out of the car BEFORE purchasing. Use free online tools to check typical failure points, recall histories, and common problems for the exact year/make/model you're considering.

56. Beware of Cars Sold "As-Is"

When it comes to the purchase, remember that YOU are buying a car that is "AS IS." This means that there are no guarantees and you assume ALL risks and ALL responsibility from the moment you give the seller your money. Please understand this purchasing style. Regardless of this purchase being "AS IS," do not deter from seeking your mechanic's insight about the vehicle. Always take the car to a mechanic FIRST. With private sellers and small lots especially, "AS IS" means there is no legal recourse later if something breaks — so inspections matter even more.

57. Check the Air Conditioning and Heat Thoroughly

Keep this in mind, older vehicles will often have automobile A/C issues. One of the seasonal problems with buying a used car is most people buy many of their used cars in the spring and summertime. And as a result of that, you may not know if the heat works well in the winter time. If winter is not the time of year you are purchasing offline, and you cannot check the heat and this matters to you, then be cautious. The same is true for the A/C. Both heat and the A/C may be clues into the comfort factor that you'll encounter or not encounter when buying a vehicle. People sometimes like to hide the fact that the car's A/C or heat is not working. Be sure you take the time to check the A/C and heat. Both of these can be costly to fix. That's why it's important to know what runs the heat and A/C. If either system doesn't blow strongly, it could indicate deeper issues with the blower motor, blend doors, or compressor.

58. Use Research to Strengthen Negotiation

Research the car that you want AND do research on its competitors from the same time period. This information can significantly help your search, and it most certainly can give you negotiating power. If you can get a better car that's virtually the same price, with better reliability, better mechanics, more comfort, etc., then pick the better car at the same price, or use it as leverage. Comparing similar models also gives you a strong argument when sellers overprice their vehicles compared to the market.

59. Compare Cars Within the Same Categories

When you compare, compare ALL aspects of the vehicles that are in the same price range and that are in the same category. Compare price. Compare color if you want to. Compare reliability. Compare miles driven on the odometer. Compare the car's aesthetic look. Compare the age of the vehicle. The less money you have, the more you MUST be willing to be flexible and make reasonable compromises.

Many people look at the model of a car, but rarely do people look at the miles on the odometer, or they don't take the time to thoroughly consider what their personal needs are and what they need from the car they want to buy. Do not ignore comparing aspects of the car in this process. You can also compare market prices on multiple platforms to confirm whether the seller's price is reasonable.

60. Pay Attention to the Humble Daily Drivers

Focus on regular everyday sedans and daily drivers. A 10+ year old sedan can still be an awesome vehicle for you based on YOUR parameters. Focus more on reliable everyday cars and less on heavy duty sports cars, less on large pickup trucks, and less on big unique SUVs. Why? Because each of these latter categories can cost you several thousands of dollars if you repair anything related to the suspension, the engine, the wiring, transmission, or other components vital for the car. When you are shopping for a cash car, be keenly aware of the choices you make based on your parameters. Again, this point speaks directly to prioritizing your NEEDS first. These humble daily drivers also tend to have cheaper insurance, maintenance, and parts, which matters when buying with cash.

61. Avoid Cars With Unusual Modifications

You want to avoid cars with obscure aftermarket modifications when you buy a cash car. Things like funky exhaust pipes, funky wheels, colored racing wheels, souped-up engines, weird tuning, weird gauges, racing bumpers, racing spoilers, aftermarket weird gearshifts, etc. are all signs that the car may have been driven hard or treated roughly. Some of these cars may look appealing to the eye, but the weirdness of what you are looking at means the chances of the car being tampered with or being "souped up" in weird or obscure ways is high. Avoid these types of cars and these types of sellers at all costs. Weirdly customized cars are a big NO-NO and your radar should be on high alert. Even subtle modifications—like lowered suspensions or tinted aftermarket lights—can indicate harder driving or future repair complications.

62. Be Skeptical of Sellers Who "Don't Know Much About Cars"

If the seller doesn't know much about the car, leave immediately! You mean to tell me, you owned this car for 1, 2, 3, 4, or even 5 years and you don't know a thing about it?? They may have only had the car for six months or less and they just want to "get rid of it." Be cautious about this person. This person may be trying to get rid of a problem. Ask them many questions. You want to know as much as possible about the car they are selling. Remember, they have the information, and you want as much of it as possible and you want it up front. Online, sellers often pretend not to know history to avoid admitting issues — treat vagueness as a red flag.

63. Ask Why They Are Selling the Car

Ask why the seller is selling their car. Don't skip this step. There may be no REAL way to verify the answer to this question, but this can tell you a lot about the motives of the seller. You have to get very good at having these conversations with sellers. The more conversations you have, the better you can pick up what people are really saying, how they are saying it, and what their motives really are with regard to selling the car. If their answer contradicts anything in the listing, or seems scripted or generic, dig deeper.

64. Ask for Service and Maintenance Records

Ask sellers what the service record looks like. Ask about the maintenance record on the car. Ask about the timing belt if the car is older. Some people are very good record keepers. They will keep records of all the oil changes, trips to the mechanic, and have all of the work done on the vehicle documented for safekeeping. If that's the case, then good for you and good for them. Unfortunately, many people are NOT good record keepers. Keep in mind, if they have been the owner of the car for a short period of time, they may not know about the previous owner's maintenance records. Some people may become irritated with you for asking all of these questions for the service records. That is ok with me. Ask anyway! Photos of receipts or digital service histories (common with newer dealerships) can also be helpful, so ask if they have any.

65. Check for Physical Copies of Important Paperwork

Ask to see the service records and receipts if they have them. Ask to see the car title if they have it. Ask to see the car registration as well. If they don't have these items, they should state clearly why they do not have these important items with them. Always ask for these documents even if you know they may not have them. If they are not available or are missing, write down that information and move on. Later, use this lack of documentation as leverage for the price when you negotiate. This is a crucial step because people that truly care about their vehicles keep records of the car for a reason. Be sure to ask for these important documents! If the seller refuses to show the title until purchase, that is a red flag; at minimum, they should show you a photo with matching VIN information.

66. Ask What Repairs the Seller Has Already Done

Ask the seller what they have repaired on the car and what repairs they have done since purchasing the car. Ask the seller what mechanical issues they have experienced in the car and how often they have had to repair the vehicle since owning it. Ask the seller, in their own words, how faithfully they have taken care of the vehicle while owning it. If they replaced the battery, alternator, radiator, or other key systems recently, ask why — sometimes new parts mean recurring problems.

67. Ask Specific Questions About the Engine and Transmission

Ask when the transmission was flushed or serviced. Ask when the oil was last changed. Ask when the brakes were last replaced. Ask when the oil pan gasket or the valve cover gasket was last changed. Ask how many miles the tires may have left. Ask about every mechanical, electrical, and aesthetic functioning of the car. Many people love questions. Some people hate questions. Ask anyway. The goal is to get answers to your questions. The more information you have the better and the safer you will be in this process. If the seller gets irritated or becomes defensive when you ask these specific questions, consider that a red flag.

68. Ask About Additional Owners and Car History

Ask not just how many owners the car had, but HOW MANY OWNERS DID THEY know the car had? Notice the difference in the questions. You are asking them to tell you what they know about how many owners the car may have had. They may not know for sure. Ask how long they've owned the car. If the story they give doesn't line up with the Carfax/AutoCheck report, be cautious — inconsistencies usually mean someone is hiding something.

69. Ask About Garaged Cars vs. Outdoor Cars

Ask where the car was stored. Ask if the car was garaged or left outside in the elements most of the time? A garaged car usually has better paint, better condition overall, and doesn't have the sun damage that outdoor cars have. Never underestimate the effects of weather on a car. Excessive cold, wind, and sun affects cars differently. However, overall, a garaged car is a "win" when it comes to an older used car. Garaged cars also tend to have less rust underneath, which is a major advantage in older vehicles.

70. Ask Whether the Car Was Driven Daily or Occasionally

Ask the buyer if the car was driven daily or if it was driven occasionally. Daily drivers may have experienced regular wear and tear, but sometimes occasional cars may have problems too. A car that sits in one place for several months at a time, without some type of regular driving, will usually have more problems than meets your eyes. Although older cars that are daily drivers will likely have increased mileage, they typically have fewer problems, less wear and tear on key systems, and fewer bad issues, overall. That's why "daily driver" cars make excellent used cash cars. If the car has very low miles for its age, verify that the odometer readings across records match — unusually low miles can sometimes indicate rollback.

71. Ask How Far the Car Has Been Driven Recently

Ask the buyer how far they have driven the car in the last 2 months. Many people work from home and don't drive their cars very often. If a person says that they have driven their car 25, 50, or even 100 miles to work per day, and that is their job, then their mileage "may" be fairly accurate. Oftentimes, people will quote thousands of miles per month, but that is because they want to inflate how far they supposedly drive their car to justify the mileage that is on the car. People are normally truthful on this question. If the seller hesitates, or gives vague answers like "just around town," ask more questions — vague mileage patterns can indicate the car sat for long periods, which creates its own problems.

72. Ask About the Longest Trip They've Taken in the Car

Ask how far they have driven the car and what is the longest trip in the car that they have driven recently. If you are purchasing a cash car for $3,500, and they tell you that they drove the car from California to New York and back, then that is good mileage. That trip is too far and too extensive to lie about. It also tells you that the car can take a long-distance trip at high speeds, and this information is beneficial to a cash car buyer. What you want to know is if the car is a dependable type of daily driver based on what the seller is telling you. If they claim major recent road trips, ask about oil changes, tires, or repairs done before and after the trip — it helps verify their story.

73. Ask How Frequently They Drove the Car

Ask how frequent they drove the car weekly, and how far they drove every day. If they loathe talking about this, ask if they drove the car daily, every other day, significantly on the weekends, or any pattern of how frequently the car was on the road. Ask if the car breaks down frequently, or if they feel comfortable driving the car based on their own words. Ask if the car could start up easily in the morning. Ask if the car ever left them on the side of the road recently. Ask! Draw out this information at all costs. Their answers will often clue you in on major problems. Their level of comfort in answering these questions (or discomfort), suddenly becomes the selling point in your mind. If they seem unsure or contradict themselves, that's a sign they haven't driven it much or may be hiding reliability issues.

74. Ask About Mechanical Problems They've Experienced

Ask the seller what problems they experience with the car on a weekly, monthly, or even yearly basis. Have they experienced numerous problems or very little problems with the car? Ask them if the car has shut off on them recently, or if they have had to get the car towed recently. Ask the seller if the car smokes when it starts, if the oil has had to be changed constantly, or if there has been an oil leak in the car. These answers are clues to the history of the car. If their responses are vague ("just normal stuff"), press for specifics — honest sellers usually answer clearly.

75. Verify the Seller's Story Against the Carfax/AutoCheck

Question the seller about the CARFAX® vehicle history report or Autocheck® report. If you decide to generate these reports, the things that the seller has told you should roughly match what the vehicle history reports show. If the things that the owner says don't match what the vehicle history report says, then immediately move on. You cannot trust people that cannot be trusted. A person could have bought the vehicle a short time ago, and a recent CARFAX® or Autocheck® report may not reveal any information on the vehicle. This is possible. It takes time for these large vehicle systems to update their vehicle history records. If the seller discourages you from pulling a report or says "it's not necessary," treat that as a major red flag.

76. If Anything Seems Off — WALK AWAY

Trust your gut. Trust your intuition. These car buying tips are for your best interest. If something doesn't feel right about the car, about the buyer, or about ANYTHING, then WALK AWAY IMMEDIATELY. No questions asked. No regrets. Cut your losses and move on. There are LOTS of cars for sale. No need to jeopardize your safety. No need to feel guilty about not buying a car that you may seem to like. There will ALWAYS be another car out there for sale. Use common sense and intuition to guide you through this car buying process. You have ALL the power when you are a cash buyer! Your instincts matter more than anything — and in today's world where scams and misrepresentations are common, trusting your intuition can save you from huge financial loss.

CHAPTER SIX
HOW TO BUY A HYBRID OR EV THE SMART WAY

Buying a hybrid or an electric vehicle with cash is different from buying a traditional gas-powered car. You can absolutely get great value, but you have to understand what you are stepping into. Hybrids and EVs offer benefits, but they also come with specific risks, long-term costs, and questions you cannot afford to overlook when you are spending your own money.

This chapter is not meant to turn you into a battery expert or a mechanic. It is designed to give you the practical knowledge you need so that you do not make a costly mistake. The same principles from the earlier chapters still apply — patience, research, inspection, and common sense. However, when you are dealing with hybrids and EVs, you need a few extra layers of awareness.

Let's walk through what matters most.

Understand What You Are Really Buying

When you buy a hybrid or an EV, you are not only buying a car. You are buying a battery system. That battery is the heart of the vehicle. Modern hybrid and EV batteries can last a long time, but they do not last forever. And when they do fail, they can be expensive.

A regular gas engine gives you signs when something is wrong. You can hear noises, smell leaks, or spot vibrations. Battery systems are different. They can fail slowly or suddenly without the same kind of warnings. Replacement costs can range from a few thousand dollars to well over ten thousand dollars depending on the model.

This does not make hybrids or EVs bad choices. Many of them are extremely reliable. You just need to understand what makes them different before you spend your cash.

Hybrid Batteries vs. EV Batteries

There is a big difference between the battery in a hybrid and the battery in a full electric vehicle.

Hybrid Batteries

Examples: Prius, Camry Hybrid, Accord Hybrid

- Smaller battery packs

- Less expensive to replace

- Known for long life

- Supported by a gas engine

- Easier to maintain and diagnose

Hybrids have been around for a long time. The technology is proven, replacement options are easier to find, and repair costs are usually more reasonable. This makes hybrids one of the safest choices for cash buyers.

EV Batteries

Examples: Tesla, Nissan Leaf, Chevy Bolt, Mustang Mach-E

- Large battery packs

- Much more expensive to replace

- Performance depends heavily on battery health

- Sensitive to extreme hot or cold climates

- Battery age affects driving range

EVs can be fantastic when the battery is healthy. When the battery is worn down, the range drops and the useful life of the vehicle shortens. Cash buyers have to be very careful here. A great looking EV is not a deal if the battery is near the end of its lifespan.

The Most Important Question: How Old Is the Battery?

The age of the battery is more important than the age of the car.

A ten-year-old hybrid with a newer replacement battery can be a great buy.

A newer EV with an original, worn-down battery may not be a good buy at all.

When evaluating a hybrid or EV, always ask:

- Has the battery been replaced
- When was it replaced
- Was the replacement a brand new OEM battery, a refurbished battery, or an aftermarket battery
- What is the current battery health rating
- Are there service records documenting battery care

These questions matter because the battery determines the real value of the vehicle.

How to Check Battery Health

You can get an idea of battery condition by asking for service records, but you can also use diagnostic tools.

For hybrids, many shops can run a health report that shows how each battery cell is performing. This is money well spent. For EVs, battery health often appears on the dashboard or through the manufacturer's app. You want to know the current range, how quickly the range has dropped over time, and whether the car has had charging problems in the past.

If a seller avoids your questions or cannot provide clear answers, move on.

Climate and Battery Life

Batteries have a harder life in extreme weather.

In hot climates:

- Batteries degrade faster.
- Charging creates more heat.
- EV range tends to drop sooner.

In very cold climates:

- Charging slows down.
- Range temporarily drops.
- Long-term battery life can shorten if the car is regularly exposed to freezing conditions.

This does not make hybrids or EVs bad. Just remember that climate and temperature play a major role in how long a battery lasts.

Charging Habits and Their Impact

For EVs especially, how the previous owner charged the car tells you a lot.

- Charging to one hundred percent every day shortens battery life
- Fast charging all the time speeds up battery wear
- Storing the car fully charged for long periods can cause degradation
- Letting the battery drop to very low levels often can also shorten its life

If the seller cannot explain their charging habits, that should make you cautious.

Choosing the Right Hybrid or EV for a Cash Buyer

If you want:

- efficiency
- low long-term fuel costs
- reliability
- proven technology

A hybrid is usually the best choice, especially for cash buyers.

If you want:

- zero gas

- quiet driving

- smooth acceleration

- modern features

An EV can be a great choice, but only when the battery is healthy and the price reflects the remaining life of the battery.

If the battery is questionable or the price seems too high for the condition, walk away.

Sometimes the best buy is still a well-maintained gas car with a solid maintenance history. The goal is not to chase technology. The goal is to get the most reliable car your cash can buy.

Common Hybrid and EV Red Flags

You want to walk away if you see:

- sudden drops in driving range

- warning lights related to the battery

- poor charging history

- overheating issues

- sellers who avoid battery questions

- cars priced suspiciously low

- high mileage EVs with the original battery

- no maintenance documentation

When buying hybrids or EVs with cash, uncertainty equals risk. Do not gamble with a battery pack.

Hybrids and EVs can save you fuel money, run efficiently, and last a long time. They simply require a different type of attention. Focus on battery health, climate history, charging behavior, and maintenance records. Combine that with the patience and wisdom you have learned throughout this book.

The key is simple. Do not guess. Know.

When you understand what you are buying, you set yourself up to make a smart decision with your cash.

CHAPTER SEVEN
THE MOST COMMON SCAMS
(AND HOW TO AVOID THEM)

Buying a used car with cash gives you freedom and leverage, but it also requires awareness. The same market that offers great deals also has people who take advantage of buyers who are in a rush, unaware, or too trusting. Scams today often look more polished than they did years ago, but the principles behind them are the same. Someone is trying to separate you from your money without giving you a legitimate car in return.

This chapter is designed to protect you. When you know what to look for, you stay in control, avoid costly mistakes, and walk away before anything goes wrong. You cannot rely on luck when buying a used car. You rely on preparation, observation, and patience. The scams you will read about here are common, avoidable, and easy to recognize once you understand how they work.

Let's break down the scams you are most likely to encounter and how to protect yourself every single time.

Online Listing Scams

Online platforms make it easy to reach private sellers, but they also make it easy for scammers to create fake listings. These fake ads often use photos stolen from legitimate sellers. The prices are usually much lower than normal to get your attention.

Signs of a fake listing include:

- A price that seems too good to be true
- Sellers who refuse to talk on the phone
- Sellers who cannot meet in person
- Listings with no real details about the car
- Pressure to pay a deposit before meeting

The solution is simple.

Do not send money to anyone you have not met.

Do not give deposits to someone you have not seen.

If something feels off, trust that feeling.

Seller Refuses to Meet or Keeps Delaying

A common scam involves a seller who always has an excuse for why they cannot meet. They may say they are out of town, in the military, in the hospital, or working out of state. They promise the car is "perfect" and insist on a deposit to "hold it" for you.

This scam works because people want to believe they are securing a good deal.

Protect yourself by remembering this rule:

A seller who cannot meet you in person is not a seller you should be dealing with.

If they want your money before you see the car, walk away.

Fake Vehicle History Reports

Some scammers send fake vehicle history reports that make a bad car look clean. They hope you trust the paperwork without verifying anything yourself.

Always run your own vehicle history report using a reputable service. Do not trust screenshots, PDFs, or links the seller provides. Anyone can create a fake report, but they cannot fake the information when you check it yourself.

Deposit Scams

Scammers often ask for a small deposit to "hold the car" until you can meet. Once you send the money, they disappear. Even honest-looking listings can be part of this scam.

Never send deposits.

Never send money before seeing the car.

Never pay to hold a vehicle you have not inspected yourself.

If a seller is serious, they will simply move on to the next buyer without asking you for money upfront.

Curbstoning (Unlicensed Sellers Pretending to Be Private Owners)

Curbstoners buy cheap cars with problems, clean them up just enough to look presentable, and then sell them as if they are private owners. They often say the car belonged to a family member, a friend, or someone who "just moved." They try to make the sale sound simple and personal.

Curbstoners often:

- Refuse to put their name on the title
- Do not have service records
- Cannot explain the car's history
- Want fast cash with no questions asked

Always check the name on the title. It must match the person selling the car. If it doesn't, walk away.

Title Washing

Title washing happens when a damaged or salvage vehicle is moved from one state to another to remove the salvage status from the title. A car that was once considered a total loss suddenly appears to have a clean title.

This scam is dangerous because it hides the true history of the car.

Protect yourself by:

- Comparing history reports from multiple sources

- Checking the VIN carefully

- Asking direct questions about previous damage

If something is unclear, do not move forward. Good cars have clean histories. Bad cars hide them.

Odometer Rollbacks

Digital odometers can still be tampered with. A car advertised with low mileage may actually have much more wear and tear than what the odometer shows.

Signs of odometer fraud include:

- Worn brake pedals and steering wheels on low-mile cars

- Mismatched service records

- Mileage that does not line up with the car's age

- Obvious interior wear that does not match the odometer reading

Always compare the mileage with the condition.

The numbers must make sense.

Mechanical Masking

Some sellers temporarily fix problems just long enough to sell the car. They may reset warning lights, use additives to quiet engine noises, or warm the engine before you arrive to hide issues that appear during a cold start.

This is why you always:

- Request cold start and warm start videos
- Ask questions about warning lights
- Pay attention during the test drive
- Consider getting the car inspected

A seller who tries to hide something is not someone you should buy a car from.

Pressure Tactics

Scammers and dishonest sellers use pressure to rush your decision. They may claim another buyer is on the way, the car must be sold today, or they need the money urgently. Pressure exists because it works on people who are impatient.

As a cash buyer, pressure tactics do not work on you unless you allow them to.

Take your time.

Ask your questions.

Walk away if you feel rushed.

There is always another car.

Buying with cash keeps you in control, but only when you slow down and stay aware. Scammers rely on speed, emotion, and trust. Protect yourself by following the steps you have learned, checking every detail, and never sending money before inspecting a car in person.

When you stay patient, alert, and confident, these scams become easy to spot. You do not need to fear the market. You simply need to understand it.

CHAPTER EIGHT
MY CAR PURCHASES

In this final chapter of the book, I am going to give you a list of 19 cars that I have acquired over the years. Seventeen of them I've purchased, and 2 of them I helped a close family member purchase. I want to also provide you with a little detail about the cars, such as the year, make, model, how I acquired it, and what happened to the car.

Of the 19 cars on this list, only 1 of these cars actually failed because of mechanical issues. Of the 19 total cars, 2 were gifted to me, and 17 were purchased by me. Also, of the 19 total cars, 13 were purchased with cash, and 6 were purchased with a loan and subsequent car payments. As of the writing of this book, our family has not had a car payment in about 13 years, and it's been extremely liberating!!

Here is the list of my car purchases in order of the year the car was manufactured:

1. **1977 Toyota Corolla** – A brown stick shift – This car was gifted to me in 1994 by a friend's parents. I traded it in shortly after I got my first job as a teacher right out of college in 1994.

2. **1978 Ford Granada** – A light blue 4 door – This car was a cash purchase in 1986 from my brother for $500. It was wrecked and totaled in 1987 by someone other than me.

3. **1978 Buick Century** – A white 4 door – I took over the car payments of $100 per month from my mother in 1987 when she purchased another vehicle. The motor locked on me after I attempted to change my own oil and I used the wrong oil filter. All of the oil leaked out on the way to Western Auto, a local car repair shop.

4. **1982 Pontiac Bonneville** – A big blue 2 door – This car was a cash purchase in 1992 for $300 from my sister and brother-in-law. This car worked sporadically and eventually stopped working while I was away at college. It had multiple mechanical issues when I purchased it but I attempted to make it work my first year away at a 4-year college at Kansas State University!

5. **1988 Ford Escort** – A red 4 door – My only brand new car that I ever purchased. I purchased this in 1988 with a 5 year 20% interest loan. It had a nice factory AM/FM radio/cassette player, but no air conditioner. I had to choose between a cassette player and A/C. Needless to say I spent lots of hot summers in this car. I let my mother take over the payments when I went off to college at Kansas State University in 1992.

6. **1992 Ford Taurus** – A gray 4 door – I got a loan on this car when I purchased it in 1995. This car was stolen from me when I left it running in my girlfriend's driveway in 1997. It was later found in a shopping mall parking lot with stolen merchandise in the front seat. I had already purchased another car when it was found.

7. **1992 Toyota Corolla** – A brown 4 door – This car was purchased in 1996 by my girlfriend (now wife). We married in 2000 and this was one of our family's first cars until 2003. We made payments on it and paid it off early. In 2003, we sold this car to a nephew.

8. **1996 Honda Civic** – A green 4 door stick shift – I purchased this car in 1997 after my Taurus was stolen. I got a loan and made car payments. I had this car for a long time and ultimately I gifted this car to charity in 2008.

9. **1997 Ford Escort** – A red 4 door – Gifted to my daughter in 2013 by her Granny B. My daughter drove it throughout college until she graduated in 2017. This is the car I drive today.

10. **2002 Toyota Camry** – A gray car that was purchased with a loan in 2003 for about $19,000 from Enterprise Rental Car. This is the most expensive car I've ever purchased. This car was lost in a car accident in 2018. We owned this car for 15 years and put over 360K miles on it.

11. **2002 Toyota Corolla** – A black 4 door – This was a cash purchase in 2013 for $4,800. This car was lost in a car accident in 2017.

12. **2004 Toyota Corolla** – A red S-model 4 door – This was a cash purchase on January 1, 2015 for $5,300. This car was sold to my nephew one year later for $3,000.

13. **2007 Toyota Camry** – A gray cash purchase in 2017 for $6,400. This car is still in my family and being driven today.

14. **2007 Toyota Camry** – A red cash purchase in 2019. This car was purchased for approximately $7,400. I helped my niece and her husband make this purchase. It is still being driven by my niece and her husband today.

15. **2008 Toyota Tundr**a – A white regular cab long bed pickup. This truck was purchased for $8,400 with a loan in 2010. This truck was lost in a car accident on Christmas Eve 2015.

16. **2007 Toyota Corolla** – A gray 4 door. This was a cash purchase in 2015. This car was in an accident when a utility truck ran into the back of it. Great car, except the AM/FM radio did not work.

17. **2009 Toyota Camr**y – A white 4 door. This was a cash purchase in 2018. We continue to drive this car today.

18. **2016 Toyota Camry** – A white 4 door purchased in 2017 for $12,500. My daughter purchased this one with cash, and I helped her with the search.

19. **2015 Toyota Camry** - A Crème Brûlée Mica 4 door Sport SE model.

CONCLUSION

Buying a used car with cash is one of the clearest, most practical ways to stay in control of your money. It protects your future, lowers your stress, and gives you the freedom to make decisions on your own terms. Everything you've read in this book was written to help you slow down, think clearly, and move with confidence through a process that often feels overwhelming for most people.

You've learned how to plan, how to save, how to understand the market, how to talk to sellers, how to protect yourself from scams, and how to evaluate everything with a steady, patient mindset. You've also seen how these ideas played out in my own life. None of this is theory. These are real steps that work in the real world.

If there's one message I want you to carry with you, it's that **you don't have to rush.**

Good deals show up when you're prepared.
Good decisions happen when you take your time.

And the best outcomes come when you trust what you see and stand firm on what you know.

Cash gives you choices.
Cash gives you leverage.
Cash gives you peace.

And now that you understand how to use it wisely, you're in a stronger position than most buyers on the road today. You don't need perfect knowledge to buy a good used car. You just need a plan, patience, and the willingness to walk away until the right opportunity shows up.

As you start your search, remember: you're not just buying transportation. You're making a financial decision that affects your daily life, your future savings, and your overall peace of mind. Treat the process with the same level of seriousness and respect you'd give to any important investment.

You're ready now.
You have the tools.
You have the awareness.
You have the confidence.
And you have the cash.

Move wisely, trust your preparation, and enjoy the freedom that comes from making a smart, disciplined, well-informed purchase. The next keys you hold won't just belong to a used car — they'll belong to a decision you made intentionally, patiently, and with full control.

And that's the whole point.

ABOUT THE AUTHOR

Eric Bowie (Smart Money Bro) is a personal finance educator, YouTuber, and founder of *Smart Money Bro®*, a movement dedicated to helping everyday people make, save, and invest more money with purpose. After rebuilding his finances from negative net worth to millionaire status, Eric now teaches practical wealth-building principles that work in the real world — not just on paper.

Through courses, books, coaching, and content, *Smart Money Bro* helps people manage their way to financial freedom — one intentional step at a time.

With more than half a million YouTube subscribers, over 40 million views, and a growing online community, *Smart Money Bro* is known for his no-fluff approach to money management. As a self-made, modern-day voice for wealth building and financial discipline, his message is simple yet powerful: *"The best person to take care of the old you — is the young you."*

www.ingramcontent.com/pod-product-compliance
Lightning Source LLC
Chambersburg PA
CBHW060629210326
41520CB00010B/1537